Robert Fulton's Steamboat

by Renée C. Rebman

Content Adviser: Allynne H. Lange,
Curator,
Hudson River Maritime Museum

Reading Adviser: Alexa L. Sandmann, Ph.D.,
Associate Professor of Literacy,
Kent State University

Compass Point Books ✦ Minneapolis, Minnesota

Compass Point Books
3109 West 50th Street, #115
Minneapolis, MN 55410

Visit Compass Point Books on the Internet at *www.compasspointbooks.com*
or e-mail your request to *custserv@compasspointbooks.com*

On the cover: Robert Fulton's steamboat steams up the Hudson from New York
City to Albany on August 17, 1807.

Photographs ©: The Granger Collection, New York, cover, 12, 22, 27, 34; Prints Old and Rare, back cover (far left); Library of Congress, back cover, 37, 40; Mary Evans Picture Library, 4, 23, 30; Independence National Historical Park, 6; Bettmann/Corbis, 7, 25, 33; North Wind Picture Archives, 9, 15, 19, 31, 35; Collection of the New York Historical Society, USA/The Bridgeman Art Library, 16, 20, 24; Historical Picture Archive/Corbis, 17; Central Library, Birmingham, West Midlands, UK/The Bridgeman Art Library, 29; Darlington Memorial Library, University Library System, University of Pittsburgh, 36; Architect of the Capitol, 39; Private Collection/Peter Newark American Pictures/The Bridgeman Art Library, 41.

Editor: Julie Gassman
Page Production: Ashlee Schultz
Photo Researcher: Eric Gohl
Cartographer: XNR Productions, Inc.
Library Consultant: Kathleen Baxter

Art Director: Jaime Martens
Creative Director: Keith Griffin
Editorial Director: Nick Healy
Managing Editor: Catherine Neitge

For my son, Roderick, and my daughter, Scarlett

Library of Congress Cataloging-in-Publication Data
Rebman, Renée C., 1961–
  Robert Fulton's steamboat / by Renée C. Rebman.
      p. cm. — (We the people)
  Includes bibliographical references and index.
  ISBN-13: 978-0-7565-3351-9 (library binding)
  ISBN-10: 0-7565-3351-1 (library binding)
1. Fulton, Robert, 1765-1815. 2. Steamboats—History. 3. Marine engineers—United States—Biography. 4. Inventor—United States—Biography. I. Title. II. Series.
  VM140.R8R36 2007
  623.82'4092—dc22   2007003941

This book was manufactured with paper containing
at least 10 percent post-consumer waste.

TABLE OF CONTENTS

"FULTON'S FOLLY"

Hot sunshine beat down upon the boat dock, located just a few miles north of New York's City Hall. A long, thin boat fitted with two enormous paddle wheels on its sides rested in the water. Its innovative steam engine sent puffs

Though a number of guests were invited, Robert Fulton considered the maiden voyage of his steamboat a test run rather than a social event.

of thick black smoke up through its chimney. The date was August 17, 1807. Though few realized it, history was being made.

Amazed, the crowd watched as a group of about 40 men and women, dressed in their finest clothes, boarded the boat. Their finery was quickly blackened by smoke and small burns from the soot raining down. Onlookers in the crowd jeered at "Fulton's Folly." No vessel they had ever seen had been powered by an engine. They expected the boat to blow up once it began to move.

A signal was given, and the steamboat began to move. It went only a short distance before stopping. The passengers, nervous and irritated, complained. One passenger said, "I told you so; it is a foolish scheme: I wish we were well out of it." Robert Fulton, the man who designed the boat, spoke briefly to the crowd and then adjusted the machinery.

In a very short time, just after 1 P.M., the paddle wheels churned through the water, powered by the steam engine. "Fulton's Folly" began its maiden journey, up the

Hudson River to Albany, New York. It soon left New York City behind.

The voyage lasted through the night, and at 1 P.M. the following day, the steamboat made its first stop, near Germantown, New York. It pulled into a private landing that was part of the Clermont estate owned by Robert Livingston, Fulton's business partner.

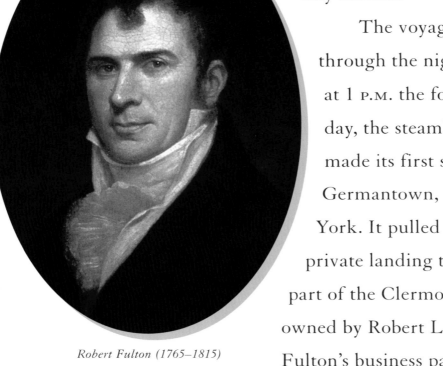

Robert Fulton (1765–1815)

In high spirits, Livingston greeted the passengers. They stayed ashore overnight.

The next morning, joined by Livingston, the passengers reboarded the boat and continued on to Albany. An amazed crowd, which included the governor of the state,

6

The average speed of Fulton's steamboat was nearly 5 miles (8 km) per hour.

hailed their arrival.

The boat made the 150-mile (240-kilometer) trip in record time: only 32 hours. Robert Fulton declared the journey a success, stating that steam would give access to the great rivers, "laying open their treasures to the enterprise of our countrymen."

Newspapers of the day barely mentioned the trip. A brief editorial in the *American Citizen*, a New York City daily paper, offered congratulations to Fulton and declared that the steamboat "cannot fail of being very advantageous." This would prove to be a glaring understatement. Fulton's steamboat ushered in a new era of transportation.

Before the steamboat, goods and people were transported by sailboats, flatboats, and keelboats. But each of these early boats had obvious disadvantages.

Sailboats depended on the wind for power. Without wind, sailboats had to be rowed, if possible, or towed. Flatboats were made to float downstream only. Upon reaching their destination, the flatboats were often broken up and the lumber reused for building projects.

Keelboats were propelled by boatmen carrying long, iron-tipped poles that were pushed against the bottom of the river. When the water was too deep for the poles,

In the 1800s, flatboats were often used to move freight on America's rivers.

the boatmen attached long ropes to the boat and walked onshore, pulling the keelboat along. Keelboats also couldn't be used on rivers with strong currents, such as the Hudson, because the currents could cause the boatmen to lose control.

The steamboat was an amazing improvement. It was much heavier and larger and could handle the currents of bigger rivers. It also had much more speed. However,

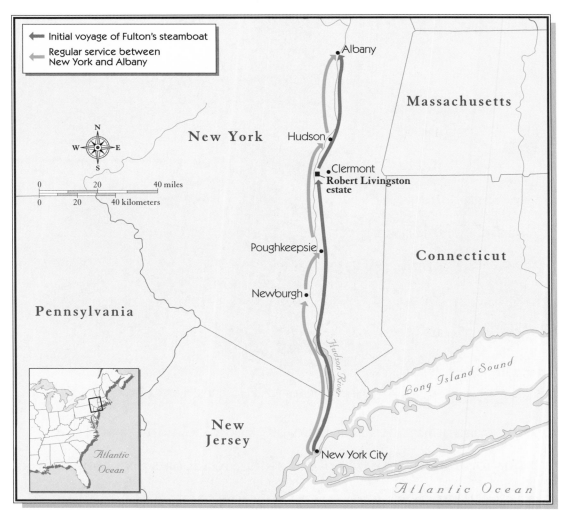

Fulton's steamboat made three stops during its regular service route.

steamboats began to force many boatmen out of their jobs.
Crewmen working on steamboats had to know about
engines and mechanical repairs. Boatmen were not happy

with the arrival of the steamboat.

After the first successful voyage, Fulton and Livingston immediately began offering regular steamboat trips up and down the Hudson River. Life on the river changed quickly. People could travel in less time, and goods could be shipped faster. Steamboats had a big impact on many businesses. Merchants could now sell their products to more customers in far-reaching areas.

Fulton's *Clermont*, as the steamboat was later called by the press, ushered in a new era in shipping. Modern transportation speeded the growth of American cities. Families could settle where they liked, knowing they could still get the items they needed to run their households. Steamboats pushed the young nation into an exciting, fast-paced future.

IMAGINATION AT WORK

Robert Fulton was curious and imaginative, even as a young boy. He was born in 1765 on a farm 20 miles (32 km) south of Lancaster, Pennsylvania. The first seven years of his life he

The birthplace of Robert Fulton is recognized as a National Historic Landmark.

enjoyed the country, but his father, Robert Sr., fell deeply in debt. The elder Fulton was forced to sell the farm and almost all of the family's belongings. He wrote, "Y have Nothing to By Land Back Nor money to settup with in town."

In Lancaster, Robert's father returned to his former occupation as a tailor. After his death only two years later, the family was so poor that some of the five children were sent to live with relatives. Robert tried living with an uncle but soon returned to his mother. She tried to raise him properly.

Robert attended a strict school, and the lessons did not always hold his interest. In order to keep his attention, his teacher sometimes physically disciplined him. After being hit on his hands with a cane stick, Robert cried, "Sir, I came to have something beaten into my brains, and not into my knuckles."

The curious boy much preferred to conduct his own studies. He made lead pencils and household utensils for his mother. He performed so many experiments with the liquid metal mercury that he earned the nickname "Quicksilver Bob." Robert also discovered he had a strong artistic talent. Many of his watercolors showed great promise.

When he was 10 years old, the American Revolutionary War began. The city of Lancaster was transformed into a supply center for the Continental Army. Troops stopped to rest and load up on supplies. Soldiers swarmed the streets. Prisoners of war crowded prison encampments.

Gunsmiths kept busy trying to keep the Army supplied with weapons. Robert often hung around the gun shops, learning their methods. His quick mind absorbed all he saw. He also put his artistic ability to use and made many mechanical drawings for the gunsmiths. Robert learned enough to make an air gun, which fires ammunition with compressed air. The inventor in him had already taken root.

Robert's family still struggled for money. Around 1779, his mother had him apprenticed to a jeweler in Philadelphia. In exchange for Robert's help, the jeweler

Gunsmiths used some of Fulton's suggestions in their gun designs.

taught the boy metalworking, miniature painting, and hair weaving. Robert spent hours carefully working the hair into detailed decorative designs and jewelry pieces. He also did sign painting for businesses to earn extra money.

Robert began to specialize in miniature portraits. These were extremely popular because cameras did not yet

Miniature portraits were often worn as pieces of jewelry.

exist. People wishing to have a picture of a loved one to carry in a small case or to preserve in a locket had to have a miniature painted. Robert eventually opened his own shop.

His business was one block away from the Delaware River. He watched the ships travel the water daily. The young man did not yet dream of boat building. Robert Fulton was determined to become an artist.

EUROPEAN ADVENTURES

Looking forward to a new career, Fulton packed his art supplies and traveled to London. He arrived during the summer of 1786. Fulton was full of confidence, and he carried letters of introduction from influential friends. The letters helped him become acquainted with artist Benjamin West. Originally from Lancaster himself, West helped

Letters from his friends helped Fulton make a favorable start in London.

17

Fulton find lodgings. Fulton studied under West and soon learned that the life of an artist was not an easy one.

Fulton lived frugally and often had trouble paying for the room he rented in a boardinghouse. Getting mail was another expense. In those days, the recipient, not the sender, of a letter paid for the postage. So Fulton asked his mother to use very small writing and thin paper, saying, "If you can send me a pound of news upon an ounce of paper I shall save almost a guinea by it."

In 1791, two of Fulton's paintings were exhibited at the Royal Academy. Even this honor failed to gain him any significant orders for paintings. However, his natural charm did enable him to move in upper-class circles. Fulton met the Earl of Stanhope, and their common interest in mechanics led to a long friendship.

Stanhope was an inventor who had his hands in many projects, steam power being one of them. He had designed a steam carriage as well as a steamboat. Neither design was ever built. Stanhope had studied the steam engines

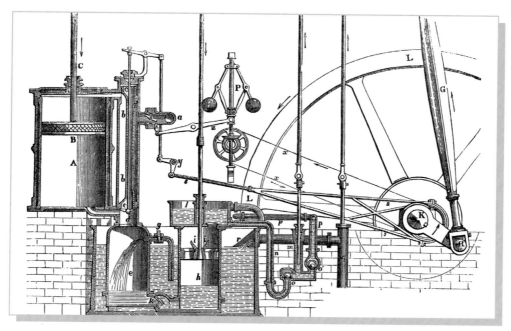

James Watt, of Boulton and Watt, designed a steam engine that used double action. Steam was pumped at each end of a cylinder to drive the piston back and forth.

built by the firm of Matthew Boulton and James Watt in Birmingham, England. This may have deeply influenced Fulton, because the focus of his career changed from art to civil engineering and inventing.

Another society friend, the Duke of Bridgewater, got Fulton interested in canals. These man-made waterways were used to ship goods. Fulton published a book in 1796 titled *Treatise on the Improvement of Canal Navigation*.

One of Fulton's drawings featured an incline to carry a boat to an upper canal.

It contained 17 drawings of inclined planes, boats, and aqueducts. It also included many calculations about speed of vessels and water resistance.

By 1797, Fulton decided to look for further opportunities in Paris, France. There he met a fellow American, Joel Barlow, an author, statesman, and scholar. Barlow invited Fulton to live with his family and tutored him in mathematics and physics. Fulton picked up his brushes once more and painted his friend's portrait. Fulton also had a new idea. He wanted to build a submarine.

Fulton hated war, and he became convinced that if a

submarine could be fitted with bombs, it could sneak up on enemy ships and destroy them before they could make an escape. He hoped that if nations realized such powerful and destructive vessels existed, it would stop them from launching attacks on each other.

Submarines were not new inventions. In fact, one had been used during the Revolutionary War, but without much success. Fulton knew he could make a better submarine. His design was called the *Nautilus*.

In order to support this project, he created a huge painting titled *The Burning of Moscow*. But this was no ordinary painting. He erected a large domed building where huge canvasses, twice as tall as a man, were mounted on concealed rollers. The paintings were unrolled as if by magic, making the story come alive. Called a panorama, this form of entertainment was very popular in a world in which motion pictures and television did not yet exist. Fulton made a big profit from his panorama.

He used the money to build the *Nautilus*. Fulton's

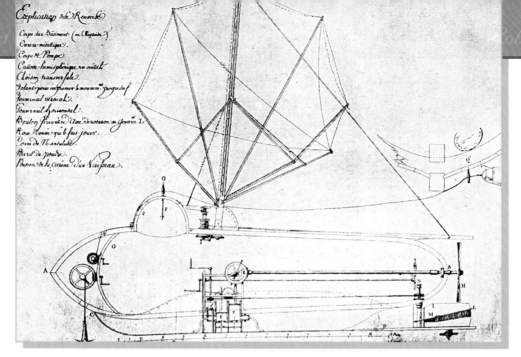

The Nautilus *featured a sail, so the vessel could be steered on the surface. When the submarine was submerged, the sail folded back.*

submarine had impressive features. Tanks of compressed air provided oxygen to a crew of two or three men so they could stay submerged for long periods of time. A periscope allowed them to view activity at sea level while they were underwater. The *Nautilus* could also launch an attack.

During the summer of 1801, Fulton gave a demonstration in the French port of Brest. He used the *Nautilus* to send a torpedo into a large single-masted sailboat called a sloop. The sloop was destroyed. Many people were impressed, and French Emperor Napoléon Bonaparte expressed interest in the vessel. But, in the end, he did not order the building of any submarines. Fulton felt the sting of failure.

His luck soon changed. Early in 1802, Fulton met Robert Livingston, the U.S. minister to France. Appointed by President Thomas Jefferson, Livingston had a long and

Fulton met with Napoléon to present his plan for French submarines.

important career in American politics. He had served as secretary of state from 1781 until 1783. He had also served on the committee that wrote the Declaration of Independence.

Livingston was extremely interested in steamboats. He had obtained a 20-year monopoly to provide steamboat

23

Robert Livingston (1746–1813)

service in the state of New York. To keep the contract, he had to produce a steamboat within one year. He knew Fulton was the man to help him accomplish it. He persuaded Fulton to give up submarines and work on steamboats with him.

Fulton had been criticized for not offering his submarine to the United States. He believed his arrangement with Livingston would go far to ease hurt feelings in his home country. He said, "I am bound in honor to Mr. Livingston to put my steamboat in practice and such an engine is of more immediate use to my country than submarine navigation." His words would prove correct.

BUILDING THE BOAT

Fulton's steamboat was constructed at a shipyard on the East River in New York. It was moored in the water beside the workshop of Charles Brownne, who was in charge of its building.

Not everyone supported the project. Angry boatmen plotted revenge. Under the cover of darkness, vandals made

Fulton took his first steamship out for trial runs on the Hudson River.

their move. Steering their own boat through the water, they rammed against the hull of Fulton's boat. They hoped to cause serious damage and put a stop to steam power, which endangered their livelihood.

The damage could be repaired, but Fulton was forced to take steps to protect his property. In his expense account, he made this entry: "$4.00 to the men for guarding the boat two nights and a day after the vessel ran against her." This type of vandalism occurred many times, but Fulton would not be stopped. He knew his boat would change the way people traveled and make him and Livingston a nice profit.

Steamboats were not new. Twelve patents had already been granted for other American steamboats. In fact, in 1763, American gunsmith William Henry had built a steam-powered vessel.

Then in 1790, John Fitch built and operated a passenger steamboat on the Delaware River. It carried paying customers between Philadelphia, Pennsylvania, and Trenton, New Jersey. Ultimately, Fitch could not make

26

John Fitch's steamboat featured canoe-type paddles.

enough money from the venture and stopped his boat
service. Some people believed it was impossible to make a
steamboat with enough power to travel quickly and carry
passengers safely.

27

Now, in 1806, Fulton was determined to accomplish what no other man had. He studied designs that had failed and improved upon them. He made his boat long and slender. This streamlined design made for less friction and resistance, so it improved speed. He also made many changes in the shape and placement of the paddle wheels to get the best results. Fulton did not believe an inventor had to have a completely original idea to be successful. He believed an existing idea could be altered and improved to benefit mankind.

He watched as his design took shape. His boat was 146 feet (45 meters) long and 12 feet (4 m) wide. Its flat bottom and straight sides provided stability. There was a large, uncovered paddle wheel on each side to propel the boat forward. The height inside the cabin was 6 ½ feet (2 m)—"sufficient for a man with a hat on," Fulton said.

Fulton and Livingston shared the building costs. They paid Brownne $1,666 to build the hull. The Boulton and Watt engine Fulton wanted was expensive. It cost

$2,750. Shipping and storage added another $5,122. The engine worked by cycling hot and cold steam inside a main cylinder, pushing a piston up and down. This motion, called a stroke, powered the attached paddle wheel. It was the most powerful and efficient engine available.

Less than a month after the steamboat made its successful maiden voyage, Fulton registered the craft as the *North River Steamboat*. It began making regular runs up and down the Hudson.

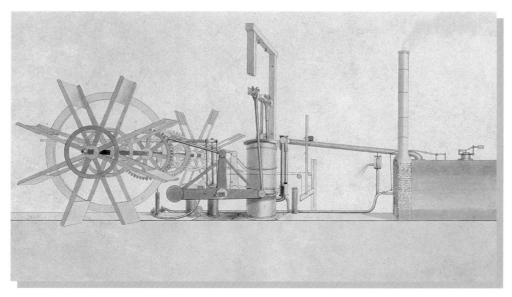

Fulton asked Boulton and Watt to modify its typical engine design. He provided a diagram to show what he wanted.

STEAM IS KING

Traveling on the *North River Steamboat* from New York to Albany took about 32 hours and cost $7. In contrast, taking a stagecoach took 60 hours and cost $10. The traveler making the journey by sloop, a popular sailboat of the day, could count on spending one to seven days on the water. Those brave enough to board the steamboat in 1807 saved both time and money.

While on board, passengers were provided with meals, and there

Before the steamboat became popular, sloops were the main form of transportation on the Hudson River.

were 12 sleeping berths. Light cargo was stowed and transported. The *North River* ran her route until the river froze in mid-November. Fulton and Livingston made $1,000 in profit during the first three months of their venture. It was enough for the pair to see a bright future.

Fulton gathered the most experienced crew and workmen to operate the boat. They had to be able to run

Fulton's steamboat sailed past a steep line of cliffs, known as the Palisades, on its route.

the engine and handle any repairs that might be needed. They were paid well, and Fulton made the men feel as if they were part of an important group. With a strong crew in place, it was time to improve the business.

Over that first winter, the *North River* was completely rebuilt. The partners invested another $4,000. The boat was made 7 feet (2 m) longer and 4 feet (1.2 m) wider, with a new deck and windows. In anticipation of more passengers, it was fitted with 54 sleeping berths. A new kitchen, pantry, bar, and boiler were added.

Because renovation was so extensive, Fulton had to reregister the vessel. On official papers, he registered it as the *North River Steamboat of Clermont*, perhaps giving a nod to his partner's estate. Referred to as the *Clermont* by the press, Fulton never called his steamboat by that name. He always simply called it the *North River*.

Proud of his elegant new boat, Fulton posted strict regulations to keep it shipshape. "As the Steam-Boat has been fitted up in an elegant style, order is necessary to keep

The North River *was an average size boat, however its engine made it both heavier and faster than other boats of the era.*

it so," he declared. According to his rules, gentlemen were to "observe cleanliness, and a reasonable attention to not injure the furniture." Smoking was forbidden except in certain areas, and all card games and other recreation were to end by 10 P.M. so passengers could sleep undisturbed.

Soon passengers became accustomed to the convenience of traveling by steamboat, and the vessels grew to accommodate them. Over time, they became much more elaborate than Fulton's first steamboats.

33

In 1811, the Paragon *became the third steamboat built for the Hudson River service.*

In 1808, Livingston approached the New York state legislature to revise the terms of his 20-year monopoly. The legislature agreed to add five years to the contract for every boat the men put on the water, for up to 30 years. This gave them another decade of control. The partners could also seize any steamboat operating illegally and collect a penalty. Over the next few years, they built several more boats. Fulton and Livingston had conquered the Hudson River.

FULTON'S LEGACY

The years after the success of the *North River* were extremely busy ones. Livingston negotiated an agreement to operate steamboats on the Mississippi River. He was granted rights to a 300-mile (480-km) stretch beginning at the mouth of the river in New Orleans and continuing north to Natchez, Mississippi.

The Louisiana Purchase of 1803 had doubled the

In the Louisiana Purchase, the United States bought 828,000 square miles (2,152,800 sq km) of land from France for about $15 million.

size of the United States and opened the West. The country was growing rapidly as pioneers settled new areas. The Mississippi River was vital to shipping and trade.

Fulton designed a new style of steamboat with a paddle wheel positioned at the stern, or rear of the boat, instead of one on each side. Too busy managing his other boats and business concerns, he hired Nicholas Roosevelt to oversee the construction. Roosevelt's shipyard was in Pittsburgh, Pennsylvania, along the Monongahela River. In 1811, the

At the time that the New Orleans *was built, Pittsburgh was not yet an industrial center. Steel production became important for the city following the War of 1812.*

boat was completed. Fulton called it the *New Orleans*.

The boat's first journey was quite an adventure. Roosevelt, his pregnant wife, their dog, and a full crew took the craft west on the Ohio River and then down the Mississippi. A few weeks into the 2,000-mile (3,200-km) journey, Roosevelt's wife gave birth on board. Also, the *New Orleans* survived a fire and a strong earthquake. It reached its destination, however, and was soon carrying passengers.

Fulton built a warship named the *Demologos*. Paid for by Congress, it was the first steam-powered vessel ever built for the U.S. Navy. It was launched on October 14, 1812, but it never

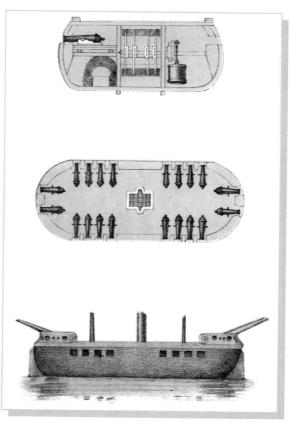

The Demologos *was also known as* Fulton the First.

saw battle. The War of 1812, between the United States and Great Britain, ended before it was ever called into service.

Fulton's later years were marred by legal battles. Other inventors applied for patents on steamboats, forcing Fulton to defend his designs. He also went to court numerous times when businessmen challenged the Hudson River monopoly. The courts always sided with Fulton. A lifetime of perseverance gave him strength to hold his ground.

On a cold winter day in January 1815, Fulton and three friends were trying to return to New York from a business trip to New Jersey. Because no ferries were running, Fulton hired a private boat to take them home.

The shallow water near the New Jersey landing was frozen, and the boat could not reach the shore. The four men were hurrying across the ice of the Hudson River toward the boat when a sharp crack sounded. The ice had broken. Thomas Emmett, Fulton's lawyer, slipped into the treacherous freezing water. Fulton and the other two men

sprang to action and some-
how pulled him to safety.

The men made it
home, but Fulton suf-
fered from exposure. His
doctor was called to his
home. The doctor reported
Fulton was hoarse and
"almost unable to articu-
late." Fulton revived and
shortly thereafter insisted
on taking another trip to
Jersey City, New Jersey,
to check on a boat being

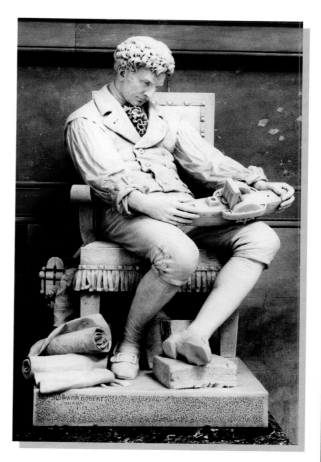

A statue of Robert Fulton sits in the U.S. Capitol.

built. However, he soon fell ill with pneumonia and died on
February 23 at 49 years of age. He was survived by his wife,
Harriet, and four children.

Newspapers carried notices of Fulton's death out-
lined in heavy black borders. His funeral procession, in

New York City, was attended by huge crowds. To honor him, guns were fired from ships in the harbor. He was buried in a Livingston family vault.

Fulton was a man of great intelligence, curiosity, and charm. He was a new type of inventor, improving on existing ideas by using the latest technology. His greatest invention, the *North River*, left its mark on travel, commerce, and legislation.

A replica of the North River *was built in 1909 in honor of the 300th anniversary of the exploration of the Hudson River by Henry Hudson.*

Trains and steamboats, as depicted in an 1864 Currier & Ives print, coexisted for many years.

Steamboats continued to flourish even as railroads were being built in the Hudson Valley, starting in the 1840s. Use of the steamboat increased after the Civil War, but the golden age of elaborate steamboats ended around 1920. By then, the vast railroad system offered both speed and more destinations. In addition, the private automobile offered an even more convenient way to travel. These transportation methods employed the latest technology to provide what the growing nation demanded. This was something Fulton himself would have very much understood.

GLOSSARY

aqueducts—structures that permit water in a canal to flow over a river in its path

berths—shelflike beds or bunks used as sleeping quarters on boats and trains

calculations—use of a mathematical process to determine an outcome

civil engineering—a profession concerned with design and construction of public roads and bridges

compressed air—air under pressure greater than that of the atmosphere

innovative—advanced or unlike anything done before

monopoly—the right, granted by a court, to conduct business without competition

moored—secured by cables, ropes, or anchors

patent—the right to be the only one to make, use, or sell an invention for a certain number of years

statesman—a leader in national or international affairs

vandalism—intentional destruction or defacement of property

DID YOU KNOW?

- In 1965, the U.S. Post Office Department (now known as the U.S. Postal Service) issued a stamp in honor of Robert Fulton.

- A statue of Robert Fulton sits in Statuary Hall in the Capitol building in Washington, D.C. It was sculpted in 1883 by Howard Roberts. His studio was in Philadelphia, Pennsylvania.

- Robert Fulton is depicted in the elaborate paintings decorating the dome of the Capitol. The Greek goddess Minerva is portrayed speaking to Fulton and Benjamin Franklin.

- As chief judge of New York state, Robert Livingston administered the oath of office to George Washington during his first inauguration. Livingston later negotiated the Louisiana Purchase under orders from President Thomas Jefferson.

- It was a popular but dangerous practice for two steamboats heading in the same direction to race to the nearest port. By cheering, the passengers encouraged the captains to go faster. Sometimes collisions and other accidents occurred, resulting in injury and even death.

IMPORTANT DATES

Timeline

1765	On November 14, Robert Fulton is born outside Lancaster, Pennsylvania.
1779	Fulton is apprenticed to Jeremiah Andrews, a jeweler in Philadelphia.
1786	Fulton sails to England to study art.
1792	Fulton begins to study civil engineering.
1799	Fulton exhibits his panorama in France.
1800	The *Nautilus* is built.
1802	Fulton forms a partnership with Robert Livingston to build a steamboat.
1807	On August 17, the first voyage of the *North River Steamboat* is a success.
1811	The *New Orleans* is built to operate on the Mississippi River.
1812	The U.S. Navy's first steam-powered war vessel, the *Demologos*, is built.
1815	Fulton dies on February 23 at age 49.

IMPORTANT PEOPLE

JAMES WATT (1736–1819)

Partner in Boulton and Watt, whose reliable and powerful engine was a key to launching the Industrial Revolution, changing America from an agricultural society to an industrial one; Watt built his first steam engine without having seen a working model and coined the term "horsepower" for measuring the power of engines

JOEL BARLOW (1754–1812)

A close friend and supporter of Robert Fulton when he lived in France; the well-educated poet and statesman helped Thomas Paine publish his famous Age of Reason—*a pamphlet that stirred many Americans into supporting a revolutionary war against England*

JOHN FITCH (1743–1798)

Built a working steamboat before Fulton, but could not get financial support for it; a liberty ship (a mass-produced cargo ship) was named in his honor during World War II

BENJAMIN WEST (1738–1820)

Served as a mentor for Fulton when the young man went to London to be an artist; West was the first American artist to go to Europe to study; after painting King George III and other members of the royal family, he was appointed historical painter to the court

WANT TO KNOW MORE?

At the Library

Flammang, James M. *Robert Fulton: Inventor and Steamboat Builder*. Berkeley Heights, N.J.: Enslow Publishers Inc., 1999.

Kroll, Steven. *Robert Fulton: From Submarine to Steamboat*. New York: Holiday House, 1999.

Parks, Peggy J. *Robert Fulton: Innovator With Steam Power*. San Diego: Blackbirch Press, 2004.

Zimmerman, Karl. *Steamboats: The Story of Lakers, Ferries, and Majestic Paddlewheelers*. Honesdale, Pa.: Boyds Mills Press, 2006.

On the Web

For more information on this topic, use FactHound.

1. Go to *www.facthound.com*

2. Type in this book ID: 0756533511

3. Click on the *Fetch It* button.

FactHound will find the best Web sites for you.

On the Road

Hudson River Maritime Museum

50 Rondout Landing

Kingston, NY 12401

845/338-0071

A museum dedicated to the maritime history of the Hudson River Valley

Robert Fulton Birthplace

1932 Fulton Highway

Quarryville, PA 17566

717/548-2679

The restored birthplace of Robert Fulton and a National Historic Landmark

Look for more We the People books about this era:

The Alamo
The Arapaho and Their History
The Battle of the Little Bighorn
The Buffalo Soldiers
The California Gold Rush
California Ranchos
The Cherokee and Their History
The Chumash and Their History
The Creek and Their History
The Erie Canal
Great Women of Pioneer America
Great Women of the Old West
The Iroquois and Their History
The Klondike Gold Rush
The Lewis and Clark Expedition
The Library of Congress

The Louisiana Purchase
The Mexican War
The Monroe Doctrine
The Ojibwe and Their History
The Oregon Trail
The Pony Express
The Powhatan and Their History
The Pueblo and Their History
The Santa Fe Trail
The Sioux and Their History
The Trail of Tears
The Transcontinental Railroad
The Wampanoag and Their History
The War of 1812
The Wilderness Road

A complete list of We the People titles is available on our Web site:
www.compasspointbooks.com

INDEX

About the Author

Renée C. Rebman lives in Lexington, Ohio. She has written several nonfiction books for children and particularly enjoys historical subjects. She is also a published playwright. Her plays are produced in schools and community theaters across the country.